CHRONOLOGY FOR KIDS
UNDERSTANDING TIME AND TIMELINES

TIMELINES FOR KIDS
3RD GRADE SOCIAL STUDIES

BABY PROFESSOR
EDUCATION KIDS

Speedy Publishing LLC

40 E. Main St. #1156

Newark, DE 19711

www.speedypublishing.com

Copyright 2017

In this book, we're going to talk about understanding time and timelines. So, let's get right to it!

WHAT IS CHRONOLOGY?

The word chronology comes from the Ancient Greek word "chrónos," which means time. It's the science and art of arranging things in the order that they occurred. For example, if you were asked to put a series of events in chronological order, it would mean that you are being asked to order those events by the time sequence when they happened.

A GOLDEN HOUR GLASS

990   1995   2000   2005   2010   201

CHRONOLOGICAL TAPE BY
FIVE-YEAR INTERVALS

2020 2025 2030 2035

lacing events in chronological order is valuable for events of all types. Historians and scientists use timelines of all different scales. Sometimes biographies can be displayed using timelines as well.

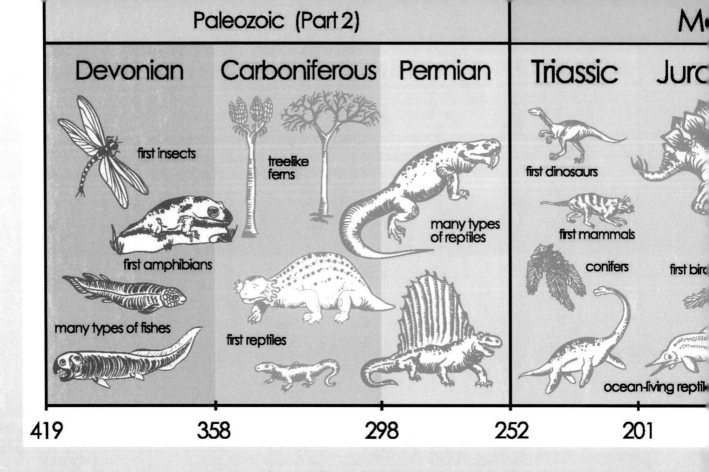

Paleozoic (Part 2)

Devonian   Carboniferous   Permian   Triassic   Jur

first insects

treelike ferns

many types of reptiles

first dinosaurs

first amphibians

conifers   first bir

many types of fishes

first mammals

first reptiles

ocean-living repti

419   358   298   252   201

WHAT IS A TIMELINE?

A timeline is a list or graphic that shows events in the order when they occurred. You can use any blocks of time when you create

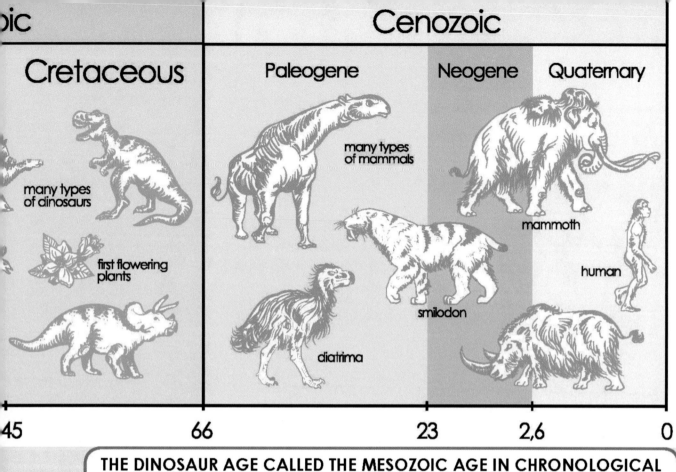

‍‍oic	Cenozoic		
Cretaceous	Paleogene	Neogene	Quaternary

many types
of dinosaurs

first flowering
plants

many types
of mammals

mammoth

human

smilodon

diatrima

| 45 | 66 | 23 | 2,6 | 0 |

THE DINOSAUR AGE CALLED THE MESOZOIC AGE IN CHRONOLOGICAL
ORDER OF THE TRIASSIC, JURASSIC AND CRETACEOUS PERIODS

a timeline. For example, if you were going to show the timeline of how life evolved on Earth, you would create a timeline that stretched over millions of years. On an evolutionary timeline, ¼ inch could represent 50 million years.

On the other hand, if you were going to create a timeline of your day from when you got up this morning to when you went to sleep, that same ¼ inch could represent just an hour or less of time. In general, timelines don't provide detailed information about events. Instead, timelines provide you a great overview so that you can understand events in perspective.

MY LiFE TiMELiNE

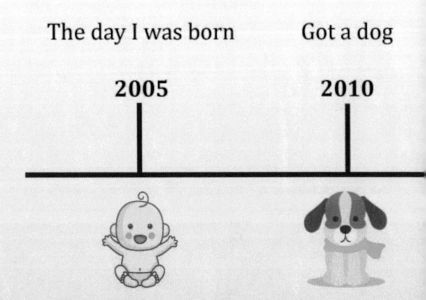

The day I was born

Got a dog

2005

2010

TYPES OF TIMELINES

There are two main types of timelines:

LiNEAR TiMELiNES

A linear timeline displays a picture of a series of events as they happened over a span of time.

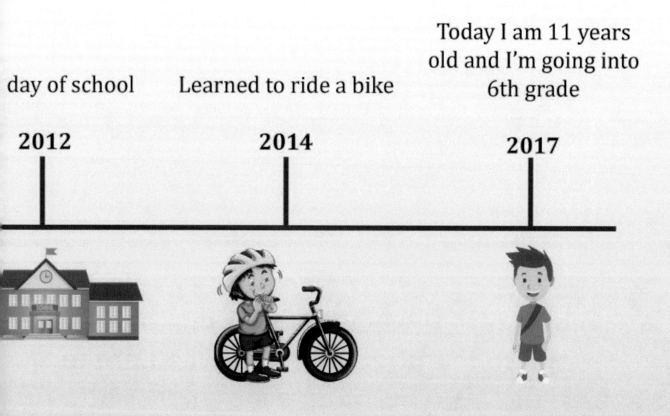

day of school   Learned to ride a bike   Today I am 11 years old and I'm going into 6th grade

2012   2014   2017

It can be displayed either horizontally or vertically. Linear timelines can be used for any types of events that take place in a sequence.

COMPARATIVE TIMELINES

A comparative timeline shows simultaneous events so that they can be studied at the same time. This type of timeline might show events that were happening at the same time in different countries, across different cultures, or across different subject areas.

HISTORICAL TIMELINE EXAMPLE

	EGYPT	MESOPOTAMIA
1000	New and Middle Kingdom	Old Assyrian Kingdom
2000	Old Kingdom Pyramids	3rd Dynasty
3000	Early Period	Akkadian Period
4000	Writing	Writing
B.C.E	**EGYPT**	**MESOPOTAMIA**

HOW TO CREATE A TIMELINE

To create a timeline, the first thing you need to do is to gather up all the facts you want to include, and place them in chronological order. For example, suppose you wanted to create a timeline of the history of the city you live in. You could start with the day the land was first discovered or the date that the first structure was built. You couldn't list every event that ever happened in your city. Instead, you would pick notable or important events.

Begin by marking the starting date on your timeline and the major event that happened on that date. Then, you would list the last event that you want to display on the timeline at the opposite end. Next, you could divide up the remaining time into equal segments. For example, you might want every segment to represent 50 or 100 years, depending on how old your city is.

Not all timelines are divided into equal segments. Sometimes a lightning bolt symbol is used to show that a period of years has been omitted because the timeline would get too large. A bracket can be used to display a span of years.

PERSONAL TIMELINE IMPORTANT LIFE EVENTS

Born	Married	Gave birth daughter	Lived in US	Lived in Canada
1965	1990	1995	2002-2007	2008

GENERAL TIPS FOR CREATING A TIMELINE

You don't have to create a complicated graphic to make a timeline. A timeline can just be a list of historical events, as long as they are in chronological order. Remember that a timeline tells a story in a concise, compressed format.

Good timelines have the following characteristics:

- They display facts and events that are well researched.
- They are organized in the correct chronological order.
- They have the most important facts for the timeline's topic.

- They are easy to read because they were planned in advance, then sketched out by hand or with a graphics program before they were published.
- They represent the time periods involved in a way that's clear for the reader. The time periods are generally proportionally correct.

- They use color to make things clear without overdoing it.
- They use blank space effectively so that everything is easy to understand.
- They generally have events listed for every date that appears on the timeline.

- They use pictures where possible to make the information easier to understand.
- They have text that is correctly spelled and in a font size that's easy to read.

STEPS FOR CREATING A SIMPLE HISTORY TIMELINE

There are some steps you should follow when creating a history timeline.

STEP 1: Decide what you want the timeline to depict. Will it show personal events? Will it show biographical events in a famous person's life? Will it show political events or historical events that happened in a specific location?

STEP 2: Research the facts that you want the timeline to contain. Then, organize them from the earliest event to the latest event.

STEP 3: Choose the overall span of time that you want the timeline to represent. It can be minute-to-minute or a span of millions of years.

STEP 4: Decide what units of time you are going to use. Not all timelines have equal spans of time, but most do. It's almost as if you are drawing a vertical or horizontal ruler and each inch represents whichever time period you want it to represent.

STEP 5: Calculate the number of total segments that you want your finished timeline to have. If you have some events that are widely spaced in time, you may want to show a lightning bolt symbol for the passage of years.

STEP 6: Sketch out the line, either vertically or horizontally, and divide it into the number of segments you need to represent the span of time you want the timeline to depict.

STEP 7: Label your dates appropriately as you move from left to right.

STEP 8: Choose the locations on the timeline where the dates fall and label them appropriately. Use color labels, icons, or codes that refer back to the chronological order. Once you pick a way to represent specific items, be consistent.

STEP 9: If you have a lot of events to list, you may want to break your timeline into smaller chunks or use categories or themes to organize it.

UNDERSTANDING TIME DESIGNATIONS ON A TIMELINE

Now that you've learned how to create your own timeline, you can practice reading more complicated timelines. As you've been studying history, you have more than likely come across the following abbreviations:

BC, which means before the birth of Christ

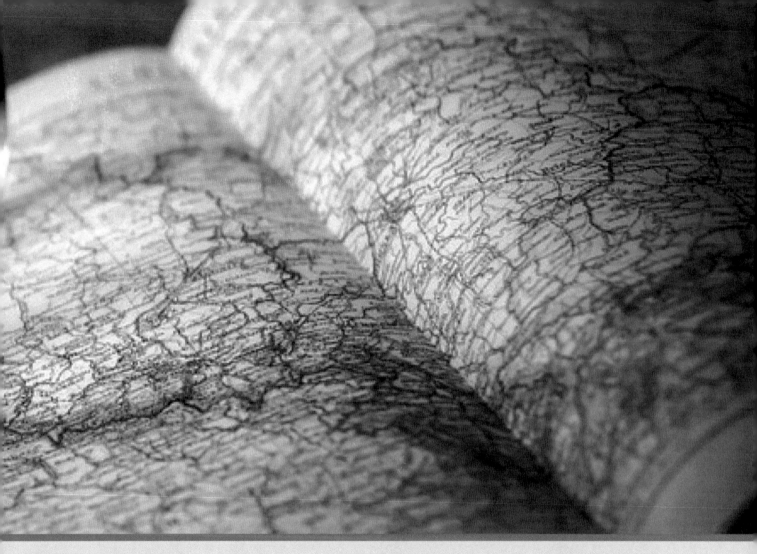

BCE, which is a replacement for BC and means "Before the Common Era"

AD, which means Anno Domini in Latin, translating to "in the year of our Lord"

CE, which is a replacement for AD and means "Common Era"

The reason these abbreviations were changed is because BC and AD refer to before Jesus was on Earth and after He was born. However, not everyone is Christian so this change reflects respect for different religions worldwide. The years designated as BCE begin with larger numbers and then go down to 0 before the Common Era begins. Once the Common Era begins the numbers go from smaller to larger.

Timelines actually make this change a lot less confusing. Another potentially confusing designation is the way centuries are listed. For example, if an event took place in the 19th century, it means that it took place sometime between the year 1801 CE through the year 1900 CE.

Horizontal timelines are read from left to right, just the way you read the text in a book. When the timeline has dates from BCE through CE, you'll need to add to get the amount of time that has passed. If the dates are all BCE, then you subtract to find out the amount of time that has elapsed.

The same is true for CE. If the dates are all CE, then you subtract to find the amount of elapsed time. For example, if someone were born in 325 BCE, in 300 BCE he or she would be 25 years old. On the other hand, if someone were born in 10 BCE and then died in 58 CE, he or she would have been 68 years old at the time of death.

OTHER QUICK TIPS FOR STUDYING TIMELINES

Before you read or study a timeline in depth, it's a good idea to scan it for these items.

- Read the title to see what the timeline is about. Not all timelines have titles but many do.
- Look at the start date and compare it to the end date to find out how much time the timeline represents.

- Determine the intervals of time that are marked on the timeline.
- Study the events that are listed and think about how they are related to each other.

SUMMARY

Chronology is the science of studying things in the order in which they happened throughout time. Timelines place historical, cultural, personal, or geological events in either a horizontal or vertical format. A simple list in chronological order is a timeline. Graphics can be used to make timelines clearer as well as more interesting. Creating or studying timelines can give you a concise overview of a subject before you learn it in depth.

Awesome! Now that you've read about timelines you may want to read about a specific timeline in the Baby Professor book *U.S. Economy in the Mid-1800s - Historical Timelines for Kids*.

Visit

BABY PROFESSOR
EDUCATION KIDS

www.BabyProfessorBooks.com

to download Free Baby Professor eBooks
and view our catalog of new and exciting
Children's Books

Made in the USA
Las Vegas, NV
27 December 2023

83601423R10040